My Dark Poetry Affair

By:

JCK

I would just like to say I am grateful to you the reader
for supporting my journey.
Thank you to all my loved ones for always believing
in me, and pushing me to continue my love of art
and writing.
It has always been a powerful outlet for me.
Especially in my darkest times.
So I encourage everyone to find a passion, hobby,
or just a healthy outlet; to help keep you motivated,
mentally strong, and emotionally happy; so it allows you to
love and live life to the fullest!

Much love
~JCK~

So it begins,
It all must begin somewhere……
The first chapter of my journey, was rather dark,
full of pain and despair.
Come into the depths of my soul.
Come into my shadows of loss and betrayal.
The death of innocence and the
beginning of true happiness
I never wish my darkness upon another soul.
Only peace and love I wish upon to all

JCK

Paint it in Blood

Drink from thee immortal beloved
Drink from thee and touch my soul.
Drink from thee divine beloved.
It is without trepidation I bare you my soul.
I am but lost here; forever yours I belong.
In darkness alone you wait no more.
My life is done here; in day light I wish to
be no more.
Turn my heart black, and tears of blood shall pour.
Save me my immortal beloved.
Save me from my soul.
Save me, my divine beloved;
Death awaits at my door.

JCK

I beg for silence........
I hear it constantly,
whispering in the darkness.
Lurking.
Ghosts altered by shadows.
Heed warning to my name.
Lurking, preying
Screaming......
I beg for silence........
I beg for silence.
Free my pain.
Such compunction I feel.
Whispering my name.
I beg for silence......
I beg for silence.

JCK

~Atrophy~

It shall come again, until a cause end.
Beat down my soul, my innocence no more.
Sores filled with sadness, blood spills to
the floor .
It shall come again, until a caused end.
Vacant filled eyes,
Devoid of all ties

Enervate my soul, my innocence no more.

Angels of the earth pray once more.
A child is lost, death knocks at
her door.
It shall come again until a caused end.

~~~~~~

JCK

My dark poetry affair.…..
So appealing, the taste so inviting.
Spiralling down, tingling numb.
Not a care, not a worry.
Only desire,
So inviting, so peaceful.…..
And then SILENCE.…………..
Sun kissed face, warm hugging breeze.
Sweet scents, so appealing.
From the depths I rise.
I see myself, with my own eyes.
Peace at last,
At last,
At last.
My dark poetry affair.….
I have peace at last.

JCK,

Past ghosts and
present profaneness.......
"The hypocrites hope
shall parish!"

JCK

Believe

I wanted to believe, believe in you.
Believe one day you could really love me.
How could you break my heart.
How could I allow you to break my heart.
Am I to blame?.......
To play the fool; is that what you see me as?
I desperately needed you.
My soul, my innocence, bruised more each day as I realised what you really were
My nightmares enter into daylight, becoming a reality.
Painful memories and images flood my eyes and pour down my cheeks.
Gasping for air, the world turn grey;
Truth washes over me, thick black tides of validity.
I wanted to believe, believe in you,
believe in me, believe in love.
I believe in hate, incestuous hate.
Save me from myself; Free me of the hate I hide.
Save me from myself, embrace my pain.
Forgive me for what I've become.
Dark whispers
Just hide away, hide the truth ; The truth of my roots, my past.
Hide the pain, accept the pain.
Believe in pain, in forgiveness;
Believe in a new day.

JCK

~I miss you~

When I close my eyes I still see you here.
Such a long time ago,
Do you remember?
Like a dream slipping away I grasp for every
piece of you.
I can still see your eyes......
beautiful like a love song.
You're fading away,
oh how I miss you.
When you left, life stood still, ended.
Such a daze of despair.
I close my eyes , and I can feel you.
In my dreams I see you.
How I miss you......
Beautiful like a love song, don't fade away.
I miss you.
Till we meet again, don't slip away.
I love you.

JCK,

INSTINCTUAL

SUCH UNREASONABLE AGONY GROWS AND BREEDS WITHIN
UNABLE TO DEDUCE SUCH INFLUENCE.
WHY............
SO MUCH FOCUS ON SO MUCH ANIMOSITY
SULLEN IN DARKNESS.
WHY............
CAN IT NOT JUST SLIP AWAY.
UNABLE TO EXPRESS CONNECTION, EMOTION.
LIKE A SWITCH, IT SHUTS OFF.
DECAYING...
UNDESIRABLE.....
MUTILATING WAYS; TO LOVE; TO FEEL.
LOVE; IMPIETY.
PHYSICAL AFFIRMATION
EMOTIONAL DESOLATION.
SEXUAL ABOMINATION
WANTING TO FEEL,
PRAYING IT TO STOP.
DEEP TURMOIL CUTS DEEP INTO MY FLESH.
I JUST WANT IT TO END.
THE ONLY WAY I KNOW, THE ONLY WAY I WAS TAUGHT.
IMPRESSIONABLE IGNORANCE
LUSTING FOR ATTENTION, AFFECTION.
THAT DISEASED DARK "LOVE".
EMBEDDED INSTINCTUAL UNHOLY ACTS .
DETACHED NOT TO LOOSE,
DISJOINED TO NOT BE ALONE
DISCONNECT TO FEEL "LOVE".

C

FOREVER ARE THE SHADOWS OF
WHO WE ARE.....
SO CLOSE THAT I CAN FEEL YOUR HEART;
SO CLOSE NO MATTER HOW FAR APART.
FOREVER IS WHAT WE ARE,
FOREVER ARE THE SHADOWS
OF WHO THEY ARE

❲ C❳

Forebearer

When it's cold outside, and I'm under your spell.
Such deep torment I feel.
Scarred from sins, spawned deep in the depths of hell.
Your face is there, burned in my mind.
Unable to erase images frozen time,
My soul feels twisted and confined.
Love fills the world,
Sanctimony took yours away.
What you should have been,
I still search for today.
The demise of my youth, it can not be
replaced.
I close my heart, I turn away, unable to bare a truth
I have faced.
Who's to blame for this hate that
grows inside.
Do not, can not, breathe your name,
Such heinous shame I hide.
Confused ; alone again. Because of you I cry.
Bleeding and broken how do I heal the child that
makes this woman lie.

JCK

Ever so quickly

Never so weakly
Not to seem ever so sickly
but it should end rather so quickly.
Breathe it in, breathe it out.
Everyday they fill you with doubt.
Slowly kill your soul
Spoiled like a rotten decaying core.
Lie awake at night
treachery I remember.
Dormant.........
Awaiting my revenge
Ever so sickly
Never so weakly
It should end ever so quickly.
Breathe it in, release it out.
Just wait until you see.....
The nightmare I have in store
for thee.......

JCK

The consumption of greater
gluttony is never enough.
More and more until
you fill your wanton cup.

JCK

No regrets, I do it all for you.
No regrets; for I fear I will only complicate you....
Do not excuse my behaviour.
No regrets, I do it all for you.
Don't flicker out...... as I fade away.
You are meant to set the world on fire.
Release all your doubts.
No regrets.
I will only take your last breath away.
No excuses for my behaviour .
It's in the palm of my hand; so set the world on fire.
Having you; you loved me; loved me knowing the darkest side of me.
I will do it all for you; only for you; always for you.
No regrets; please.
Complicate me, as I complicate you.
Don't flicker out, we will set the world on fire.

JCK

Slip in, Slip out

On the border.
Slipping in and out.
Death and life
Teetering......................back and forth.
Back and forth.
Hanging on, slipping away, hanging on.
Tic tock, tic tock.
Teetering tic ; teetering tock.
Life breathing, death still reeling.
Slip in, slip out.
Alive I see, death I stalk.
Surrounding everything, everywhere; all around me.
Corrupt my thoughts.
Tic tock, tic tock.
Tic I breath; tock I stop.
The dead march on, as the living talk.

JCK

I LIE
I CHEAT
I STEAL

I HATE
I BLEED
I HEAL

A LIFE CONDEMNED
TO FEEL

HOW CAN U
BELIEVE IN ME

WHEN I CAN'T
EVEN BE REAL

TEAR THE LAYERS

RIP THE BULLSHIT

BARE THE REAL ME

UNMASKED
UNENHANCED
UNENRICHED

RAW READY TO FEEL

THE RAW TRUTH UNDER-
NEATH
THE "TRUTH"

JCK

<u>Dark Stranger</u>

Satisfy me
I beg of you
I abdicate my status
For a moment to be lost with you
I beg of you
Satisfy me
I plead with you
Set me free
I abdicate my fortune
For a moment to be lost in your eyes
In your strength
In your arms
I abdicate my throne
Satisfy me, satisfy me.........
I beg of thee
Satisfy me

JCK

Father

I dreamt of you last night; so rare.
I cried for you; cried for me.
For what we never had.
So lost,
As I watched you, your head in your hands,
tears streaming.
Lost in limbo,
not realizing you were already gone, you reached to
me.
Are you scared? tears streaming,
In barely a whisper you reply "yes".
You are terrified and yet, yet relieved.
Don't you wish you fought?
Knowing inside, for you the thought of loosing a
fight to a lost battle
was more to bare , than just accepting it.
Sunlight crept through the windows; it's time to go
again.....
Every time we say goodbye I am more at peace.
Able to love more dead then when alive.
You can finally love the way you had always wanted.
No pain, no fear, no anxiety, no remorse.
Just peace
We finally said goodbye, I dreamt of you,
And we said goodbye.

JCK

My hour glass of life is to come to an end.
I am tired, and just wish to rest awhile.
Sail boldly into the night.
Souls will be found,
collected in the moonlight.
With not a trace, nor a sound.
Let us not fight, with nothing left to say.
We will be just fine, let us just sleep,
Let us not define
And we will be just fine.....

JCK

Haven

Write it in my blood;
Write it in water;
Write it in time.

I feel your soul as
You sleep.

Enter my heart;
Touch my soul.

Breathe in my life,
And taste me on
your lips.

Bountiful; gallant.
Fringe no more.......

Unbroken offering,
Offer your life, offer your love

Written in time,
Written in blood,
Written in tears.

Infinite and evermore;
Enclosed in your soul.

JCK

Pop another pill
Inhale a powdery tale
Consequences unreal
Unacceptable
Consume sweet poisonous nectar
Venous flow sputter....
Sputtering slow
Unstable , as opium sleepily dances
through veins.
Remedy the night,
Stupefy my mind
Powerfully numb....
Untouchable....
Untraceable
Body flow; fluid throw.
Convulsing from below
Blood pours;
Muscles let go

JCK

FORLORN

ALONE
I AM NO ONE
INVISIBLE; I DREAM OF DEATH
I LONG FOR ETERNAL DARKNESS, AS MUCH AS I
WISH FOR LOVE.
NO LONGER A VIRGIN TO REALITY
I AM A SLUT
FUCKED BY LIFE
I BLEED TRUTH AND INCESTUOUS PAIN.
LOOK INTO MY EYES AND READ MY HORROR.
MY MIND A BLANK PAGE; MY SKIN COLD AND
NUMB
MEMORIES AND LIES, BLUR INTO ONE
CONTROL IS LONG GONE
I AM WILTING IN THE SUNSET
UNLOVED; SING ME A LULLABY
SING ME A DEATH SONG

J K

Vulture Parade

Perfect bosom; perfect breast.
Heed to my wrath!
Head to ground, bow where my silk ends.
Stick to sceptre, sceptre to hand; power be now.
Forever, amen.
Heathens dance; perpetual bliss.
Your fate shall be as your mind.
Mirrored thoughts madness at will.
Greed dripped fangs;
The vultures parade.
What God do you praise, speak thy name!
How now greed, lust, and vain.
Purge blaspheme from thy soul.
No saviour of the cross would preach such foul tongue.
Recoil to the hell you once came.
Grow conscience; away from guilt.
Throw out the sceptre, disrobe the silk.
The vulture parade shall march no more.
Silence of gold, silence of power.
Dominance subdued, bereft of all senses.
The vulture parade shall march no more.
Turn away from the night, to the right hand I stay.
How now gentle shepherd, watch over as I pray.

JCK

CORE

Poison set upon a throne
A regal decadence portrayed forlorn.

Prudent and pungent,
Gallantly twisted.

Pick these scabs,
I pick these scabs to the bone.

Searching for pain
I pick these scabs, pick them to the bone.

Alone in a hell I do dictate ,
Pouring misery all over this plate.

Mountains of flesh,
It will not rest.

On this decaying throne of hate,
I pick at these scabs, pick these scabs to the bone.

A pound un-fresh,
A decaying throne of flesh.

JCK

Not as I do

Do not cause him fraught
Fallow his rules and do as he says
But "not as I do"
You must live to obey
So to others you may not engage
And do as he has taught
For he is your master

Your are on display
Sing only for him
The song bird he has encaged
His rage grows faster
So to others you may not engage.

Clipping your wings
And locking you away
Forever only his forever on display
Sing only for him
You are the song bird he has encaged

Imperfections never to be forgiven
Unattended to such puerile ways
Spiralling in the spite of an exiled gaze
Pick yourself up little song bird and turn away
This songbird undaunted by thee
Will live to sing another day.

JCK

Closer

Hemorrhage with in
Tears pour out
Unable to walk
Heart ache bleeds us dry.
So reticent I stay
As frost grows all the more
Abdicate all sense
Flushed of all morality
Complying with despair
Flesh to flesh
Ambivalent as it is
It is calling me closer
Look into my eyes
I see your story,
Do you see mine
Abandoned of all reasoning
Passion is fixed
Persisting appetites
Moreover it grows

Wary with guilt

Urged into the shadows
Forsaking my body
Surrendering to desire
Awaken a lost carnal impulse
Wanton and unrestrained
Breath to flesh
Contradictory as it is
It is calling me closer
Look into my eyes
I see your story
Do you see mine
Reticent I stay
Abandoned of all reasoning
Passion fixed
Etched in my mind evermore
It is calling me closer
Breath with breath
Lips sweet to taste
Flesh to flesh
Etched in time forever more

JCK

PéreLachaise

Afraid, and yet drawn to death.
The beauty of a tomb, of a corpse.
The shell left behind of a pure soul.
Laid on a blanket of roses.
No matter how we fight or deny;
One by one, we all fall down.
Like lemmings parading through life,
until we drop off the edge.
Without warning
We fall.....
We fallow as those before us fallowed,
to death.........we fallow.
We fallowed the fallen,
We all fall down.
To become the beautiful shell
The silent corpse
The shadow resident of a tomb
The repetitive history the living question
And yet deny
Without warning heroically, tragically,
romantically we all fall
We all fall down

JCK

Iszabelle

She fell from the sky
Sliding so celestial, and fair
False accents capture her eyes
Glitter in her hair
Perfect pout, perfect lips
Skin so silk, so supple,
And from afar....
No one can see a single scar.
Creature of night; goddess of spotlight
Fading from sight
Dancing on silver , with dreams of gold
Love; dark and thick, and cold.
Memories linger, clinging to her hips and thigh.
Reminders of love; of blue and purple disguise
Damaged are her wings
So she fell
Fell from the skies
Dancing for gold, believing in lies
Dark vacant eyes
Sight blurs from inside
As her sadness pours
She is forever restlessly caged
Yet safer to side then to hide
She stays

JCK.

It is the welcoming
of your raw inner truth.
It is being placed out into reality,
for all the world to see
And perceive.

One night, one moment
A secret I can never reveal
Only in my tortured dreams
A pain all too real
And never ending desire
A love I can never share
One night, one moment
last me a lifetime

JCK

Let it breath

Let it be my breath
 beneath the water flow
A silent hunger that grows
 ever more
With purpose and pain (doubt)
I humbly await at your door
 I await..........
Your voice a fate unknown
Let it be a gift of life.
Let it be a gift of purpose
Of satisfaction
Of fate......
Such silent frustration
Silent agony,
Such addictive torture
 and beauty
Let it breath
It grows , grows evermore
Unstoppable
Immeasurable
Unattainable

JCK

Traforare Il Fiore

Let me in and allow the world to become silent
so that I may disappear.
For I am a slave to this sanctuary
This sanctuary I worship from afar
Bringing me up from the deep
In a zombie trance I escape this sleep
How do I gain entrance
A sweet succulent small paradise
I would like to claim as my own
To touch the texture of this bountiful island
So supple and lush.
Sweet honey nectar that flows
For all eternity just for me
Like a bee to live for a queen
To suckle the sweet, and live for the feast
For I am a slave
Every moment I shall crave
Awakening me from the deep
Freeing me from my torturous sleep
Every inch I will forever worship
Parting these glistening gates; I search
Slipping perfectly through this
scintillating cove
To a premise sanctioned just for me

JCK

Eternamente

Con lei
Solo lei
Per sempre lei
Amore perso
Il mio cuore piange
Amore perso
Solo lei
Eternamente lei
Segretamente lei
Eternamente lei
eternamente

Eternamente

With her
Only her
Always for her
Lost love
My heart cries
Lost love
Only her
Eternally her
Secretly her
Eternally her
Eternally

Thank You

Thank you, for today you saved me
Saved me from being your fucken slave.
A slave to your lies
A slave to your game
My heart and mind was twisted and encaged.
Thank you and fuck you
For "letting me go" as you so eloquently would say.
As I walked over onto greener pastures,
Little did I know of all the souls you had buried below
Tumbling downward as I fell over rooted limbs
They were twisting reaching up and out to me,
Grasping , grabbing at me pulling me
To stop me from falling into my own grave
Lock me in my dungeon of despair
For I unheard the word of thee absurd
Fuck you for watching my heart sputter and sink
While knowing how I loved you; you watched it
die slowly with a smile.
Throw me on my self made bed of thorns
Lest I flow free down a river of my own blood and tears
Back from where I came.
Arising from the depths of a broken heart
I will believe again, breath again…..
Thank you for I am wiser, and fuck you for I am free.

JCK

LOUD

Standing on the corner
Just waiting to watch life
pass me by.
As my black heart bleeds dry
Past ghosts are calling.
Calling..............
Where I lay alone
Underground, not sleeping.
Past ghosts are calling
Calling me home.
The darkness is too loud
Too aware
Past ghosts are forever calling
When I am alone they are calling.
Forever calling
Calling me home
Fearful the light will turn
me to stone.
Still they will call
They are forever calling me
Calling me home.

JCK

Amore Perso

Everything becomes disoriented and unclear
My cold, strong, statuesque persona melts away.
And the only thing making sense Is to
be with you.
In your arms; forever feeling desirable.
And yet.............
Safely unattainable, and mysterious
Living for that moment, of complete surrender,
Of complete abandonment.
No morals, no rules, no consequences.
Just uncontrollable passion, want,
and never ending desire
Never have I experienced such and uncontrollable need and
hunger.
I succumb to you..... Amore Perso
Sacrificing my whole existence for a moment to
be lost in you....
In your gaze, your arms, your hands,
your mouth...........Your perfect mouth....
I am lost in you; lost from reality, lost from
responsibility, lost in fantasy.
And then I awake, awake back to reality.
I awake tortured; tortured by the thought of you.
The beginning , and the end of you.
Such sadness ..... Amore segreto......
  A silent inevitable sadness .
That I must grieve in alone

JCK

SLAIN

As she let out the blood chilling scream, you could feel her soul
spill through her eyes to the floor...
Her true beloved, knight in shining armor was no more.
With foul tongue, and lies so bold.
An art of betrayal; developed into thee art of war
You gaze into the twilight sitting on your throne............
I just wanted you to hold me and tell me I'm good enough.
My knight to King, you are no more...... With consequence blood
shall pour.
You had my world, it was all yours, but it was never enough.
So now this could be the end.............
Sitting on your throne; just praying I don't find out.
Praying for a silence of the unknown.
Give an addict a nibble and for the feast their secrets shall pour.
Perched on your throne dreaming of better days, ones that your
egotistical lust destroyed.
I just want to be there; there for you down fall.
There when you realize I was the dream you let fall.
You swore you would give it up; and now I sit crying with an
empty future in an empty home, dreaming of
 better days.
To spout I was never the queen you desired, as you fall you see
thee erroneousness of how you have wronged.

JCK

Angel of the Earth

Catch me............
A whisper in the wind; from under the moonlight; that
dances across gentle waters.
An angel on the earth lets out a cry for vigilant love.
The prayer of peace and protection is a soft murmur on a
child's lips.
In hopes it will rise again to a kingdom in the clouds;
controlled by a mighty hand that will bless this angel of
the earth.
The streams of love and dreams filled this young girls
heart.
Returning again and again, with hopes of the promise of
a new vestal day.
Black unchaste haze takes form, forlorn are the heavens
as purity is scorned.
A pale ghost lost in purgatory meadows.
Reveal your face! Cry out!
And reveal your pain of lost vernal love.
Catch me
As I pray for peace for this lost angels soul, trapped in in
purgatory meadows.
Pray for my soul, for I am the angel of the earth.

JCK

Bleeding Truth

Truth
I bleed
I bleed truth
Justice; justice
Pray.......
Forgiveness......
Facing the truth of
two lies
Broken are
these dreams
Faith?
Death of love
Pray..........
Where life and
death meet
I bleed forgiveness
Truth of consequence
I bleed

JCK

Be my vision
Be my peace
Bring me serenity
Bring me ease
I bring you my soul,
So you may watch over me
Bring me eternal life
Bring me to my knees
Be my keeper
Be my peace

JCK

My wife

I'll give you promises, I 'll create a life of make believe.

Give me your future; only I will gain.

Give me your love and I will give you my sorrow and pain.

Give me your dignity and in return I will give you only shame.

Pick you up

Kick you down

Bring you to life

Call you my wife

Wear my poisoned crown.

Give it to me, give me all of you, give me all I need.

In return I will make you bleed.

Give me confidence, I need it to breath.

Give me your soul, I need it to succeed.

Give my ego the boost it needs.

And I 'll give it all to you baby....

All the fury I need to release.

Pick you up

Kick you down

Bring you to life

Call you my wife

Tell me you love me, and I will fulfill all my needs.

Tell me you need me and I will fulfill my greed.

Watch my rise to fame and in return I will bring you pain.

I 'll fuck her, and you 'll be the one to blame.

Give me drugs, give me power, fulfill my need for fame.

I 'll tell you lies

Kick you down and lift you

  back up again.

Give me your love and

I 'll give you all my shame.

Make up a life

Call you my wife.

My poisoned crown pierce your vein.

Give me your soul and forever you will

  feel my pain.

Forever on a make believe throne

Poison is my crown piercing in vain.

JCK

About the Author

*JCK A writer and artist always wanting to push the limits outside of artistic norm.
"Its fun and necessary to break the rules at times." With a style that has been
perceived as dark ,edgy, and at times excruciatingly erotic.
JCK wants to express that beauty and art can be seen in many forms and should not
be stifled . Even in your darkest hour, beauty can be created through a
positive outlet, such as art and poetry.
A big believer in creating your own destiny in the universe; " Dream Big, and don't let
anything or anyone stand in your way!"
"Just have a back up plan! The world may not see and believe in your vision as fast as
you. But don't let that stop you. I always had a passion and love for
writing and art. But I chose school , working in the service industry and
medical field as my back up plan until my dream was ready to soar. As wise
person once told me 'Work (the back up plan) is what we do to get by, what you
do beyond that is how you become successful '.
Her pieces have been shown in shows in Canada ,Las Vegas and featured at
Agora Gallery in New York. Her art has also been published in the
Contemporary Masters book.*

*"I would rather live then dream of living"
JCK*